# FORGOTTEN WISCONSIN

## DETOUR THROUGH DESOLATION

TROY HESS

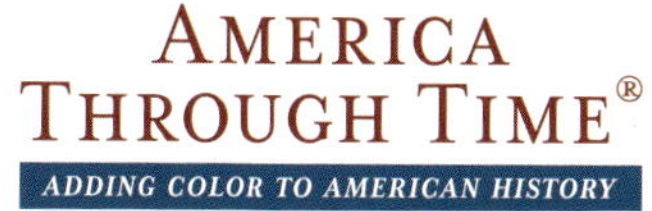

America Through Time is an imprint of Fonthill Media LLC
www.through-time.com
office@through-time.com

Published by Arcadia Publishing by arrangement with Fonthill Media LLC
For all general information, please contact Arcadia Publishing:
Telephone: 843-853-2070
Fax: 843-853-0044
E-mail: sales@arcadiapublishing.com
For customer service and orders:
Toll-Free 1-888-313-2665

www.arcadiapublishing.com

First published 2022



ISBN 978-1-63499-394-4



Typeset in Trade Gothic
Printed and bound in England

# CONTENTS

# ABOUT THE AUTHOR

**TROY HESS** is a renowned photographer and rural explorer based in Rusk County of Northwestern Wisconsin. His diverse array of images often depict colorful and dramatic imagery. His passion for photographing abandonment began with a search for a provocative subject matter. Residing in one of the poorest counties in the state, he was reluctant to find an obvious choice, as the abandonment in his area was plentiful. Over the past decade, Troy has captured the boundless abandonment littering the Rust Belt.

# INTRODUCTION

Choosing the right image for the cover was a challenging aspect of completing this memoir. The image featured on the front is a side panel of a retired fire engine. Although this volume does not entirely regard rust, it correlates to the overall subject matter. The texture of corrosion and crackling paint conveys a disposition without revealing the contents.

My objective this time is to offer a deeper look into the failed Wisconsin farmlands with a broader set of photos from my travels during recent years. I have spent countless hours studying satellite images to find where most of the abandonment remains. I then spent more of my free time driving around the state to photograph and document my finds. My only hope is to bring awareness to these fading remnants from yesteryear.

With the modest success of my first book of this genre, I received feedback from many readers. Some were upset that I did not reveal the location of each pictorial. My reason for withholding information is to safeguard against possible theft and vandalism. I chose to keep sensitive information from possibly falling into the wrong hands by not disclosing specific locations. Therefore, as a precautionary measure, the whereabouts of scenes in this publication will also remain anonymous except for public properties.

# 1

# INFERIOR INTERIORS

'm often asked, "Do you ever go in?" The answer is, I rarely enter abandoned buildings. Many are toxic tombs filled with black mold, lead paint, and asbestos. Moreso, their stability is just too unpredictable. However, there are times my curiosity gets the best of me. Occasionally I might take a peek through broken windows and open doors to see if there's anything worth photographing. Usually, these places are found in total chaos or completely vacated of belongings. On rare occasions, I find where squatters took residence inside an abandoned home.

I do not stage any of my images. What you see is the condition of how things were left when I arrived. I would also like to reiterate that the photographs within this edition are not the result of any disregard for laws or the rights of property owners.

The doorknob is rusty, and the hinges might squeak. Give the handle a turn, and let's take a peek.

Sit back and relax. It's all downhill from here. Imagine if you flee your home. How long would it take for things to decay and crumble away into a pile of rubble? I wonder how many years it takes to achieve this level of degradation. I imagine the results depend upon the duration of vacancy, as well as the structural integrity. Nevertheless, entropy ensues as degradation accumulates from years of neglect.

The interior becomes inferior when windows are left open. The mattress imperiled by time appears burrowed through by rats. A photograph tells many captivating tales. I can only imagine what happened here.

*Opposite page:* When the outside creeps in, nature swiftly consumes the contents. The leaning walls and buckling floorboards confuse the bearings. I utilized an infrared camera lens filter. As a result, the colors shift to a pinkish hue, adding to the mystery of how a room went askew.

When I drove past a derelict home, I saw a door left ajar. There were no steps for the entrance. As I approached the doorway, the floor was up to my chest. I reached upwards to knock. I said hello, but no one answered.

When the wallpaper curls away, an unsettling decor is revealed. The frail farmhouse containing this room is no longer standing.

An antique phonograph console gathers dust beneath an open window. I can imagine the room has seen better days with people dancing to the scratchy sounds of vinyl records spinning around on the turntable.

Rays of light shine through to illuminate a heap of rubble. Stains of black mold spatter the walls throughout the interior. The floorboards are weak and creak with the weight of each step. There are holes in the roof. Watch your step for protruding nails and look out for falling bits of debris.

The conversation piece is this former living room with a haphazard layout of furnishings. If only these deteriorating walls could talk. Pull up a chair and listen to the faint whispering echoes of howling winds.

Hidden in a corner was a disorganized desk with empty drawers left open. Perhaps it was ransacked by vandals in search of valuables at one time. *"If a cluttered desk is a sign of a cluttered mind, of what then is an empty desk a sign?"- Albert Einstein*

Here is a side view of a three-level home. One wall fell off, exposing the contents of each level like a cross-section. An accumulation of rainwater trickled through the roofless opening above. The dampened debris provided favorable conditions for moss and lichen to flourish.

Inside out, outside in. Sometimes it's hard to tell which way is which. This tragic outcome is the result of years of decay. Once the roof collapses, it doesn't take long for nature to reclaim the contents.

Another room where one of the walls fell off, exposing a filthy pile of rotten clothing. As I peered through the door jamb, a sharp waft of odor stung at my nose while tears of disgust reddened my eyes.

A snow-covered bathtub seems to float in a room with no floors. To capture this photo, I had to straddle a crossbeam over the basement.

I heard the roar of a bulldozer begin the disassembly of a farmhouse designated for demolition. The wrecking crew shook the house as their machinery plowed into the opposite end. As tiles fell to the floor, vermin skedaddled from the building.

Here are some ruins within ruins with a fallen barn through the window of an abandoned home. Viewing the outside gave the perception of being off-balance from within this sinking room.

## SILENT FOOTSTEPS

A dirty pair of socks lay upon a step of a dark stairwell. As creaking sounds came from the second floor, I wondered what was lurking around up there. I did not investigate the mysterious thuds any further.

The floorboards were soft from years of decay and soggy with the weight from recent rains. The floor was nothing more than an accumulation of crumbled drywall. I was unable to proceed any further into the room.

# 2

# RICKETY RESIDENCES

The following are some helpful tips on where to locate abandonment. Once you find an abandoned building, there are usually more nearby. I often encounter what I refer to as "neighbors" or "twins." These are when two or more abandoned houses are next to each other. Abandonment tends to occur near the county or state lines, as well as near landfills or graveyards. Typically, most run-down properties are within these proximities. Another place to check is down dead-end roads. Townships are less regulated and sparsely populated. There are rarely ordinances to prevent unsightliness. Dereliction usually occurs on the outskirts of townships in rural areas. When I do mapping, these are the areas I often begin my searches. My method of scanning satellite images works well for finding abandonment, saving travel time and expenses.

Another hint of abandonment is when no trespassing signs are abundant, or when there is no mailbox to accompany the property. When I notice a run-down estate, I always glance to see if a mailbox is out front. Many times the box will be lying in the ditch or missing altogether. Sometimes a mobile home or a trailer house is strategically placed to barricade a home from view. Other times the lawn is mowed to make the abandoned house appear occupied. It seems counterintuitive to keep a tidy yard for a home caving in on itself. However, these clues are usually good indicators.

# DAIRYLAND IN DISTRESS

When the world went on lockdown in 2020 for the global pandemic, the release date of my first book was put on hold for a few months. During this time, I channeled my frustrations onto canvas. The idea of the painting was to portray the scene from the cover of my first book. (Acrylic on Canvas, 16" x 20")

After completing the painting, I paid a revisit to the same residence. I was surprised to find it was still standing. Although this house is in a further state of despair, it seems livelier when encircled with summer foliage.

Lost in the sticks and surrounded by overgrowth, this old house is no longer a home.

When the location of this forsaken farmhouse leaked onto social media, the landowner flattened the home to discourage future visitors.

Eerie sounds emanated from corroded windchimes as they dangled from the eave. The disharmonious dings gave warning to the fast-approaching storm. Soon I felt a warm breeze bring cold drops of rain pelting at my forearm. With a few clicks of my shutter, I ran back to my car for cover.

A foreboding haze hovered above this forsaken farmstead. What was once a happy home now looks more like a catacomb.

The architectural style of this house is prevalent in many older homes across north-central Wisconsin.

*Left:* Rainfall drenched the dry wood of this melancholic shack. A passing cloud resembled smoke billowing from a chimney stack. I had to do a double-take to make sure this place was unoccupied. I knew the house was empty, but the smokey clouds presented the illusion of occupancy.

*Below:* It seems as though the porch is always the first to go. At first glance, one might think this would be a great fixer-upper.

*Right:* Beyond a field of daisies, there was an empty house along the tree line. The curb appeal of wildflowers is no longer welcoming to guests, only to the swarm of stinging insects.

*Below:* One of the walls fell off, and saplings grew through it.

*Left:* A crumbling home slips down the hillside in the nethers of Nowheresville.

*Below:* Wildflowers encircle this weathered woodland cottage.

*Right:* When a house settles further into the soil, it is as though it's digging its own grave.

*Below:* This north woods cabin has an unusual design. Interestingly, there was a cot lying in front of the building. There might have been an infestation of daddy longlegs to scare away the visitors from this unfavorable weekend retreat. There are plenty of pests and critters crawling into crevasses at summer cabins in the north woods.

*Left:* A tattered tarp is as good as frayed sheets. Neither works well at stopping roof leaks.

*Below:* This house is sinking. As the siding falls away, the wooden slats of the framework become exposed.

# DEADLY SHADE OF DESPAIR

A biohazardous concoction of arsenic green paint and asbestos siding comprise this toxic exterior. The arsenic vapors and asbestos dust can poison those who get too close. Black mold emanates into the mix, choking the airways of its victims with poisonous spores. Sometimes these homes are best left forgotten. I'm not sure how virulent this particular house might be. Visually this color is a good indication of toxicity, though looks can be deceiving. Proper removal and disposal of these ailing remnants from yesteryear is a costly undertaking. Perhaps another reason why most vacated homes are left for the Earth to reclaim.

Asbestos is like a bacterial pestis. The elemental glass-like fibers are combined with cement to form shingles and siding. This textile is fire-resistant, warm during the winter, and will outlast a lifespan.

In 2021, I filmed and edited a music video for "I'll Come For You" by Minneapolis-based recording artist J Desja. We obtained permission from the landowners to film at this deserted farmhouse. The ravaged interior of this former home was the ideal backdrop to portray the song. To see more of this broken beauty, please view the video on YouTube.

This house became a hollowed-out shell of its former existence.

I was wistfully awed by this weathered wooden wonder with its Old World architecture. Sadly, this place no longer stands.

I pulled over to capture a photo of this derelict dwelling while meandering along on a Sunday drive.

*Above:* In October 2020, investigators found a suitcase containing the human remains of a missing woman at this abandoned farmhouse in the outskirts of Chippewa County. Thankfully the woman was identified. Further details about this horrifying incident are still under investigation.

*Left:* I'm not sure why a barn door is on the porch here. I encounter many oddities during my rural excursions.

This two-story residence toppled in on itself.

A deserted brick farmhouse stands the test of time.

When I drove past this farmhouse, I discovered it was vacant. Sometimes it's worth turning around to take a photograph.

When the roof collapses beyond repair, all that remains is a house in despair. Most of the shingles have fallen away, exposing the interior to weather and decay.

Under the big dipper sits this former farmhouse. It was gutted out and converted into a corn crib.

# 3

# BARNS AND FARMS

There are many aging barns in Wisconsin. Not all barns are left behind, but many are in dire condition. This chapter will showcase these large rural edifices found from around the state. Some are more degraded than others. My mission for capturing these images is a means for archiving their historical context. Without lasting photographs, the history of most of these treasures will fall along with the buildings. Many of the aging barns in this chapter have long since served their purpose. It is just a matter of time before most will collapse, if they haven't already.

Sometimes when I drive past a barn, I consider stopping to take a photograph but often skip it. I later regret it when I discover the barn is no longer standing. Numerous people expressed for me to write more on these disappearing farm buildings. An abundance of barns exists in Wisconsin. Many of these buildings are thankfully still in use. According to recent agricultural statistics, there are nearly 65,000 farms in the state. And where there is a farm, there is almost always a barn or two.

## WORLD'S LARGEST ROUND BARN

Round barns are a rarity, and the World's Largest Round Barn is the king of all barns in the entire world. Although not abandoned, this building sits vacant for most of the year. Erected in 1916 for dairy cattle shows at the Central Wisconsin State Fair, it has a capacity for 1,000 people. The massive undertaking was quite an architectural achievement back in its day at 150 feet in diameter. Walking along the circumference of this behemoth is nearly 472 feet, which is longer than the length of a football field! This unique barn is a historical landmark and on the National Historic Registry. The historical status of this barn helps preserve it from the degradation faced by similar structures from the same era.

This behemoth is so immense that a wide-angle view does not capture its entirety. Here is a close-up of the main entrance. This arena-styled barn occupies the State Fair Grounds in Marshfield. It's still in use today. Let's continue our tour to discover the smaller barns throughout the region that did not fare as well.

## THE WESTERN FALSE FRONT

The facade of this horse barn resembles storefronts from the Wild West era. The architectural design cleverly disguises the roofline while making the building appear larger.

Snow-covered silos stand tall. While the barn leans further, the outbuildings soon fall.

Disheveled sheds brace together for another harsh winter.

It appears many deer went trodding up the pathway beside this barn. Those leaning walls will soon fall if they haven't done so already.

Discovering an entire abandoned farm is a rarity. Often the land is rented out for farming instead of wasting away in disparity.

Bitterly cold winds sculpt snowdrifts around a deteriorating barn. The low winter sun offers little warmth to encourage an early thaw.

As the stable becomes unstable, saplings strive to reclaim the same space.

Beneath a patch of
sugar maples and
beyond a thicket
of thorns, a broken
barn braces its final
stand against an
approaching storm.

*Left:* There is something about an antique barn in the late autumn dawn. Sometimes these old buildings make an excellent focal point in a colorful scene such as this one.

*Below:* This abandoned barn stands beside uncultivated farmlands in the middle of nowhere.

I often look for rusty rooftops when I search satellite images. The roof of this barn was easy to spot from the aerial view.

Constructed in 1927 of timber cut from the land on which it stands, this horse barn is the last of four original buildings on a large secluded estate.

*Left:* Beyond a crooked fence line, daisies absorb the sunshine. The crumbling barn bides some time as it gradually descends a hillside.

*Below:* Another barn gives way to time and decay as it leans into a grassy meadow.

This humble horse barn has a unique design.

Fieldstone masonry comprises the foundation of this classic-style barn. As with other barns of this type, stones were readily available after clearing them from nearby fields. Sadly, this barn no longer stands.

The bell rings no more as a frayed rope dangles like a severed noose in the foyer of this backwoods schoolhouse. The lead paint on the walls was vibrant in the sunlight, sealing its fate as a toxic catacomb.

This house was for sale, or at least the property was at one time. New owners leveled the disheveled dwelling and built a new home.

When deterioration sets in, it's a matter of time before the roof caves in. Once the walls begin to topple, it doesn't take long for the rest to follow.

This barn became nothing more than a wind blocker alongside a cropless pasture. What is most interesting is the wooden corn crib silo. They are uncommon to find in good condition like this one.

# 4

# CHURCHES AND SCHOOLS

In this chapter, I will showcase some abandoned churches and schools. In my first book, there were a few of these places I included. I often caught flack for not mentioning the locations. This time around, I will reveal the names and the county they reside in if they are known. As a way to discourage vandals, I won't be giving out specific coordinates to these locations. I hope my images bring inspiration to fellow explorers and to those who appreciate architecture from eras past. It was commonplace in the olden days for these buildings to serve as both a school and church.

## CLOVERDALE COMMUNITY CLUB AND KING SCHOOL (1916–1948)

The fascinating symmetrical layout of this building is now only a distant memory. In recent years it became a target for vandals and was scarred with unsightly graffiti. The dire condition of this building led to its removal on August 31, 2020. There was mention of erecting a pavilion in its place in Bayfield County.

## DISARRAY IN RAYS OF LIGHT

*Right:* In the late 1800s, settlers cut trees from the surrounding land to build this school. This log schoolhouse is likely the only one of its kind in the state. It's located on private property and far off the beaten path. I'm grateful I was given access by the property owner to wander beyond the pasture to explore this one-of-a-kind treasure. (Polk County)

*Below:* Built-in 1921, Chittamo School resides in the small Native American community of Chittamo. Classes were held here until 1950. After the generation of baby boomers, this facility lay vacant for nineteen years then used as the regional town hall until 2005. (Washburn County)

# ELMWOOD SCHOOL (LANGLADE COUNTY)

No Elm Trees grow where this hidden jewel embeds itself into the ground. In recent years, the walls bowed outward, and the roof fell into the building. It is now nothing more than a pile of rubble.

What was once a school has since become what appears to be a hunting shack. I was surprised to find this former schoolhouse deep in the north woods of Price County.

Stripped of the cross with no bell or eave, this rural church has become long obsolete. (Chippewa County)

This former school was repurposed into a storage shed. This phenomenon is a common occurrence here in the heartland. (Price County)

It's a strange time of year entering dormancy. It should be a season all to its own—the time of year after the leaves have fallen and the water has not yet frozen. Birds have migrated, and the days become shorter as the daylight dwindles. The fog brings an eerie silence before winter unleashes its fury. The mist dissipates from the ditch line revealing a mysterious school with an unknown past in Jackson County.

These crumbling stairs leading to a brick facade are all that remains. Eerily haunting, this was one of my more unusual finds. I was expecting to discover a sturdy brick building. Instead, there were only remnants of what used to be. This grand entrance to nowhere protrudes through monochromatic hues along the backroads of Lincoln County.

This former one-room school rests on the edge of marshy wetlands near the heart of Chippewa County.

A ghost town schoolhouse gathers dust from a dusty dead-end road. This school is one of the only remaining structures from one of Wisconsin's long-forgotten ghost towns. If you do your research, you may find it too. I won't reveal any specifics other than these clues. (Taylor County)

I spent several months on the lookout for this stone masonry schoolhouse. The unusual architecture is almost adobe-like, featuring large blocks of sandstone. I was glad to discover this forgotten relic hidden down the backroads where not many travelers go. (Dunn County)

## ST. JACOB'S LUTHERAN CHURCH

These stacks of crumbling bricks got lost in the sticks somewhere along the edge of the woods in Wood County.

# LOUISVILLE SCHOOL 1923

I like to call this one "Done-for in Dunn County." These older schools made of bricks are resilient to withstand the test of time. Unfortunately, this school no longer stands. Only a vacant lot remains there today.

This former church stands on the outskirts of a ghost town somewhere in Dunn County.

## SAINT ANN'S MURRY HILL MEMORIAL

Saint Ann's is a Wisconsin Historical Landmark. The church adjoins a cemetery within the Blue Hills region of Rusk County. A steep driveway veers off a dangerous curve along the highway leading up to the location. The property is maintained by locals, though decades have passed since there were services here.

## MILLADORE MIDDLE SCHOOL

Milladore is home to a massive middle school built in 1923. It seems surprisingly large for the small farming community. This former place of learning housed several hundred students during its time of operation. (Wood County)

*Right:* The etching on the plaque above the entrance reads, Meadow Brook School District No. 3, 1935. This brick beauty withstands the test of time.

*Below:* Little is known about this school somewhere along the edge of the woods in Wood County.

## CARL VON LINNE SCHOOL

"Carl Von Linne School" is the only inscription upon the plaque of this northland school along the edge of the Brule River State Forest in Douglas County.

## N. P. JOHNSON SCHOOL

This humble one-room wooden structure was the place for educating grades one through eight. It was built by the Dutch settlers of Douglas County back in the late 1800s. It served as a public school until the 1940s. During a recent revisit, I was sad to see it did not survive winter.

This monstrous structure was difficult to find as it towered behind the tree line. Farmers from a small rural community built this school in the late 1800s. Classes for grades one through four were held on the first floor, while grades five through eight attended studies on the upper level. After the school closed in the early 1960s, students merged into a larger building in a nearby school district. This monument continues to stand the test of time tucked away from view in the rolling hills of Pierce County.

*Above:* This former schoolhouse was converted into a storage shed. (Trempealeau County)

*Left:* This former country school has mud for floors and is now a pigsty. (Chippewa County)

I was excited to find this red wooden school in eastern Chippewa County.

## RING SCHOOL

The bell of this old school no longer rings.
Ironically, "Ring School" is its name. At
around 1848 feet, this particular antique
schoolhouse holds the number one spot
for being the highest elevation of former
educational establishments in the state.
I like to think of this schoolhouse as the
apogee of Wisconsin abandonment. This
historical treasure resides in the high
hills of Price County along a gravel road
leading to Timms Hill.

Strands of burned-out lights embellish the eaves of this countryside school in Trempealeau County.

## ESTONIAN EVANGELICAL MARTIN LUTHER CHURCH

The First Estonian Church built in America is far away in the backwoods. The modest chapel opened in 1914 as a place of worship for the Baltic settlers of Lincoln County. This historical landmark continues to face ongoing vandalism between various restoration efforts of recent years.

*Opposite page:* For many years, this Methodist church was the place of worship for a small farming community in Barron County. Upon first glance, some might assume this is an abandoned synagogue with the Star of David. Although the hexagram on the stained-glass window is more commonly associated with Judaism, the symbol represents the Star of Creation in Christianity. With the absence of upkeep, this church drastically disintegrates as Mother Nature reclaims it.

A shooting star gleams over the toppling entrance to this former school in northern Rusk County.

# 5

# DISESTABLISHMENTS

Large companies often outperform the ma and pa shops, leaving many no longer in operation. My extensive research of history was inconclusive for many places in this segment. Unincorporated farming communities are home to the bulk of these former business establishments. These places have become the run-down leftovers that now litter the nether regions of lost hopes and dreams.

This once-thriving general store supplied its community for many years.

"The working man's store, where you save more." This general store became apartments after the business was no longer in operation.

It was pleasant weather for window shopping at a discombobulated boutique. There was some broken glass, crumbling bricks, and a chair without a seat. A treasure trove of deals to be had right along the street.

When investments are lost, the operational costs are no longer viable.

## MELLEN STATE BANK

*Left:* Here is another abandoned financial institution. This former bank is downtown, Mellen. The stone masonry is from locally excavated rock and has words intricately carved into the stone.

*Below:* Perhaps this was a cheese factory at one time.

## CYBER MONDAY
## REPERCUSSIONS

*Right:* This old corner shop was a secondhand store and flea market.

*Below:* This former general store was the source of supplies for a small farming community. It has been vacant for many years. I was surprised at how large and warped this building was when I first saw it.

## VACANTVILLE

This small garage-like shed was once a convenience store.

Amidst the deep blue sky and snowdrifts, this boarded-up abandoned home was also a cheese factory at one time.

Fieldstone masonry forms the foundation of this former cheese house.

This former hardware store fell on hard times.

It was 39 degrees Fahrenheit one April morning at this former service garage. I was surprised to see that the temperature on the wall was accurate.

Here we have an abandoned storefront of a failed secondhand store.

In the depths of despair, amidst the frosty morning air. This building was once a town hall for a township in the outskirts of southern Rusk County.

## TOWN HALL TWO-STEP

A deer crosses my path near the old Murry town hall. Local farmers met for square dancing here at one time. This deer has the same idea and seems to use the road as a dance floor as though it's unsure of crossing.

## CORNER STOP

Just up the road from the town hall, the Corner Stop has been out of gas for a few decades now. After sitting vacant for several years, this small village convenience store no longer stands. Only an empty lot remains.

This asylum housed several patients with varying degrees of cognitive deficiencies. During the years of operation, derogatory terms such as imbeciles and idiots described the condition of residents. The nomenclature later evolved from feeble-minded to intellectually disabled as it is known today. The patients were dispersed to various adult daycare centers after this facility was no longer in operation.

It was known as The Colony, as though shrewdly implying this was a refuge designated for invalids. On the backside of the facility was the courtyard and entrance to the Recreation Room. Hereabouts is where outdoor activities likely brought plenty of smiles.

Perhaps this was a service garage at one time. It might have been the go-to place for small-engine repairs.

Here we have the deteriorating facade of a commercial duplex. These side-by-side businesses folded up sometime last century.

This retired general store resides in the northern parts of the middle of nowhere. As far as I recall, this building no longer stands.

# SPEAKEASY

All that remains of the Silver Fox tavern is this skeletal fieldstone facade. Construction began in 1936 on this bar with claims of ties to the notorious Al Capone. The structure is on the Wisconsin Historical Society website.

Old bricks crumble while thunderstorms rumble, and another watering hole goes dry. I drove quite a distance to find no records in existence. Probably a bar, but your guess is as good as mine.

The starburst molding on this tattered town hall is indicative of designs from the late 1800s. Side note, fall colors in Wisconsin are remarkable.

## TINKER-TOT DRIVE-IN

Although this property looks abandoned, it is not. The restaurant has been closed for a few decades. I thought the building and signage might offer some nostalgia to those who remember visiting here back in the day.

## EAST ARCADIA FEED MILL

The East Arcadia Feed Mill was built in 1900 and is no longer in operation. It was a two-story side-gable gristmill for housing grains. At one time, there was a water wheel to generate the power for the building. The windows are boarded up and painted to appear as window panes. Behind the mill, there is a barricade over the bridge. The signs on the fence read, "BRIDGE UNSAFE KEEP OFF," followed by a "ROAD CLOSED" sign.

# 6

# CORROSION AND RUST

"G oldmine" is the term I use to describe an area where abandonment has gone rampant. Not because there is any gold, but because there is plenty of RUST. Most often found in these less populated regions are the sweet spots littered with discarded treasures. Many of these rusting relics adjoin abandoned properties. Many old cars, trucks, windmills, and farm equipment reside in forgotten fields throughout the Rust Belt region.

From the hot and humid summers to winter's sub-zero windchill, these weathered materials endure the cycles of Wisconsin's extreme temperature fluctuations. Each slowly erodes and returns to the Earth.

Sometimes abandoned vehicles are in the driveway of abandoned properties. Other times they are left in a field to become overtaken by weeds. More often, salvage yards become the new home for these inoperable heaps. This chapter also exhibits a few other curiosities undergoing the process of oxidation.

Most old-time windmills are no longer in operation. Many times, these are reclaimed for use as lawn ornaments. This particular windmill was still spinning on a hillside along the edge of some forsaken farm field.

Brass and rust corrode to dust on this poor excuse for a Pontiac.

They say one man's trash is another man's treasure.

I discovered a Ford Galaxie lost in the brush and covered with rust. There were signs of previous attempts to revive this rear-wheel drive.

When an Oldsmobile Omega is rendered immobile, it often goes to the junkyard. Not this one. Sometimes when people inherit the real estate of a departed loved one, they do not know what to do with the belongings.

## FIELDS OF FAMINE

In the heart of America's Dairyland, a John Deere Combine rusts on the farmland it once harvested.

I often find a rusted-out clunker parked behind a barn.

A rare rustic treasure is this old-fashioned thresher. It reminds me of a mechanical elephant. On occasion, I've seen a few parked in pastures along the backroads. I do not know the year and make of this model.

The New Huber steam-powered engine tractor was a state-of-the-art marvel for the agriculture industry, manufactured from 1885 to 1903. I saw this one parked along the roadside, wasting away in the ditch line.

When a battered boat no longer floats, it becomes a lawn ornament. This display is just one of the many oddities along the northern rural roadways.

Glints of chrome and hints of rust adorn this broken-down Hudson. The Michigan-based corporation ceased production of this automobile during mid-1957. The last of its kind rolled off an assembly line in Kenosha.

Ward LaFrance was an American manufacturer of fire trucks from 1916 to 1979. Here is a retired fire engine from the Countryside Fire District. The rustic colors and textures were an inspiration for the cover of this book.

Beneath the pines and coated with grime, this atrophied Mustang is left with zero horsepower.

The flat tires on this Volvo were frozen rim-deep into the dirt.

*Opposite page:* A Chevrolet Corvair wastes away in the open air.

The headlight wasn't working. With a few shutter clicks and editing tricks, I was able to turn on the light to bring it back to life in a sense.

## CARCASSES

It's a rarity to find two similar abandoned vehicles next to each other. It appears these cars were dismantled for parts then discarded in a field.

The rarest of Wisconsin's abandoned structures are its closed bridges. This closed-off roadway crosses the Chippewa River downstream from the Jim Falls Dam. Despite the corroding beams, this failing infrastructure continues to stand the test of time. The Cobban Bridge upstream was featured in my first book and is scheduled for demolition in 2022.

The split windshield on this 1937 Ford Truck is one of the only features to identify the year of this model.

## ROUGH COMMUTE

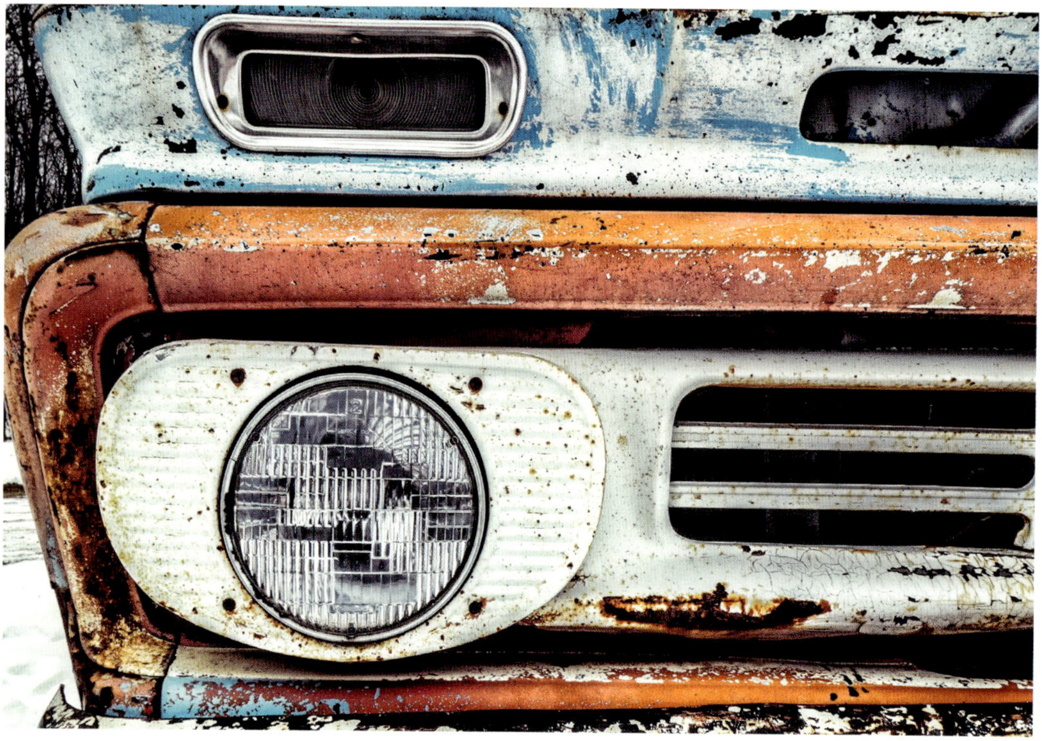

This Ford truck appears out of luck. It got stuck in some muck then discarded in a dump.

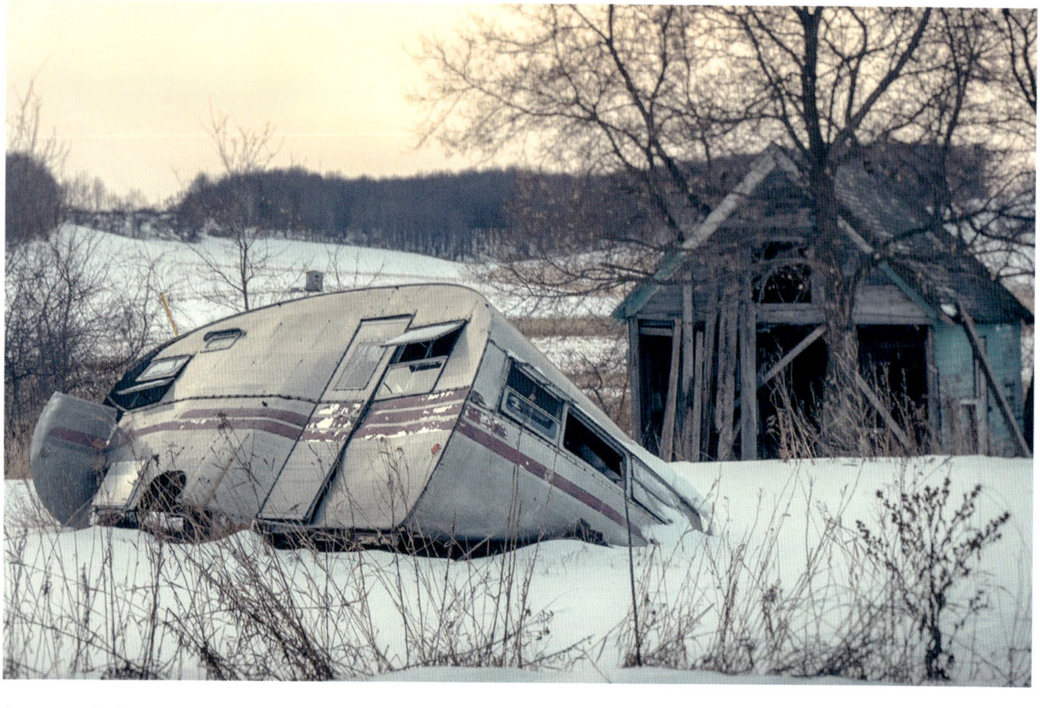

A camper is tilted off-kilter as it sinks into the melting snow.

The seeping of rust mottles the paint, consuming this group of jalopies.

When a Roadrunner no longer runs, it seems out of place in a pasture.

Someone left this trashed-out treasure parked alongside the roadside. It likely ran out of gas years ago before those patches of moss and lichen began to grow on the trunk lid. It's illegal in Wisconsin to store an inoperable vehicle within public view, even while on private property. Vehicle abandonment is a citable offense as it creates a nuisance with a list of potential hazards. Somehow this law is ignored. I can probably count a few renegades parked in the yards around my neck of the woods.

Just a reminder, there is no parking during this tour. Continue onward, just a bit further.

Another reason I refrain from revealing locations is to deter scavenging. Unfortunately, some people are only out to loot abandoned properties to strip them of valuables. Often there is a high market value on articles left behind, like this antique lightning rod with a glass insulator still intact. No one will find where this is at.

Gusts of wind rattle the corroding blades of a windmill. This simplistic contraption continues to generate power, escaping retirement as rubbish in a landfill. A little maintenance helps to keep things moving forward.

# CLOSING THOUGHTS

Wisconsin is not a state of wastelands, although plenty of abandonment prevails in the rural farmlands. My primary areas of exploration were the northern, western, and central regions. Higher concentrations of neglect exist throughout these regions. My journey was long. I drove many miles with different vehicles, and some were not even my own.

There is little hope left for restoring many of these places. I hope others can appreciate the historical significance my documentation offers. I also hope my work brings nostalgia to those who might remember some of the places we encountered.

I view abandonment as an opportunity to express art, from photography to painting to writing or producing a music video. By doing so, I bring these structures back to life by immortalizing their existence in a sense. Although some may criticize this type of work as being exploitative, I find constructive ways to revive a lost era through various forms of artistic expression. As a farewell for now, below is another example.

# SOPHIA'S WORLD

In this reenactment of Andrew Wyeth's 1948 painting "Christina's World," a young woman portrays a girl stricken with polio during the depression era. She attempts to crawl uphill through a barren field, dragging her paralyzed legs behind. In the classical artwork, she crawls towards a farm on the hilltop. In contrast, my composition is void of all structures, eliminating the likeness of a derivative. I recruited Anne Schweitzer to design the costume, who convinced her daughter Sophia to characterize the girl from the historical painting. I was delighted they both were willing to participate in this reenactment. In the months beforehand, I drove around northern Wisconsin in search of a suitable landscape resembling the terrain from the original work of art. When I found a pasture near Exeland, I knew it was a close match. We gained permission from the landowners to take photos on the land. The photo shoot did not take long. I utilized the angle of the afternoon sunlight then took a few dozen snapshots, including three instant prints. During the editing process, I digitally altered the colors to match the hues of the original painting. It was a painstaking process to cohesively balance all aspects of this image right down to the flyaway wisps of hair. The final result presents a scene that provokes a sense of hopelessness yet signifies determination through despair.

# ACKNOWLEDGMENTS

I appreciate those who support my creative endeavors. I am grateful for the out-pouring of positive support from friends, family, and people I have never met. Many thanks to each of you for joining me on this journey through yesteryear.

If this tour has left you crawling for more, please read my first two books:

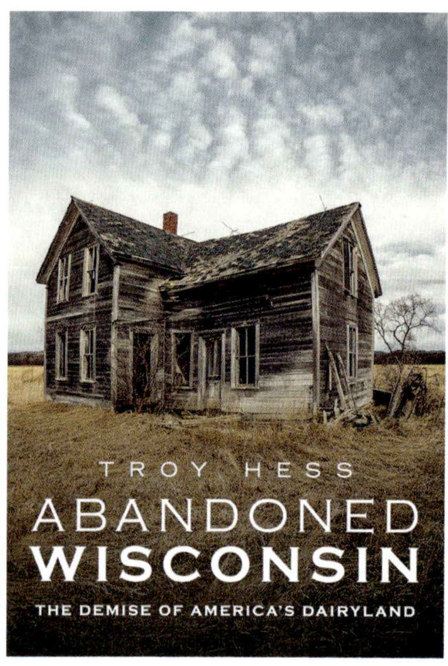

**Abandoned Wisconsin**
The Demise of America's Dairyland
978-1-63499-215-2

**Waterfalls of Wisconsin**
The Wild Waters of Intrigue
978-1-63499-370-8